I0493243

Entrepreneur-ing Series

The Prof's Guide to Going from 0 to Launch – Everything You Need to Know to be an Entrepreneur Starting Today

Second in the Entrepreneur-ing series

By: Lisa Vento Nielsen, MBA, PMP

Founder, The Next Step

www.thenextstep1234.com

Dedicated to my children Sofia and Christopher Nielsen

Table of Contents

Introduction

The first installment of this series focused on developing and using entrepreneurial skills for either launching a business OR being the boss of your career. This time, I am taking my 15+ years' experience as an entrepreneur and my 13 years' experience as an educator teaching courses on entrepreneurship to give you the Zero to Launch Guide on moving forward with your idea or your business.

This might be something you decide to do now as a full time gig or as a side gig. It might be something you want to do but are not ready to execute on *right now* – but by reading this book and using my lessons, you might decide it is something you want to do right now. You can use this book to save up for your decision in a few years – you do not have to execute and launch right now. Maybe you are just thinking and want a new, fresh look on entrepreneurship.

You are in the right place – I am a new, fresh voice on entrepreneurship using the word I coined "Entrepreneur-ING" to create a full end-to-end launch process for you to use at any time for your idea, your business and more. There is the possibility you will go through all of these steps and decide you do not want to launch but in the meanwhile you started the process. Once you start being an entrepreneur, you will always consider it again and it will help your regular full time work as you focus on making yourself stand out in this potential new venture.

I started being entrepreneurial in 2002 and I have not looked back at all. Being entrepreneurial brought an extra level of skill and focus to my other careers as educator and executive. I have tried and failed a few times and I will provide some real life case study examples based off of my own various attempts at entrepreneurship.

In this book series (and in the other series I wrote on College and Career Readiness), I am the source. My unique background and experiences and my calling as an educator mean I am pulling it all together to tie in the process from start to finish with you here in this book.

I launched The Next Step in July 2015 and for the first time, I was at a point where my age and experience had caught up with my vision. I put my face, my name and my content/writing into this business. I write books now, too and have always dreamed of being a published author so if this business has done nothing else, it allowed me to achieve a major dream of my life.

That is not all, though, all of the lessons I have learned over the years through trial and error and as a professor on this very topic have now allowed me to help you do the same process and do it well! I look forward to being on this journey with you to go from Zero to Launch with your business idea!

In Chapter 1, we will discuss business ideas and execution. It is a good high level applicable discussion on how to move forward with an idea and also on identifying ideas. Business Plan Overview is discussed in Chapter 2; the meat and potatoes so to speak of this book is going to be compiling and completing the business plan as we review it in this book. There are tons of services and templates out there but this book will take you through the steps with your own professor/consultant (me) helping you do these steps.

Chapter 3 talks about websites because you cannot have a business today period without a website. It is as natural as breathing that people will look for your website before they even consider speaking to you and you can be right in front of them and this would still happen!

As a marketing major in undergraduate and someone who is always marketing myself either through my business or other ventures, I have a lot to say in Chapter 4 about Marketing.

I go into social media in Chapter 5; this is something I have taught myself from the ground up. I am not "digitally native" and had never used Twitter or Instagram until I relaunched my company in July of 2015. I have found lots of success with using social media to drive traffic to my site without spending any money on marketing the site. As someone who has launched business prior to social media, I can tell you this is an amazing thing to be able to do. I get between 1500-2000 people per week on my site;

this is amazing for a small business that launched just eight months ago.

Chapter 6 discusses how to get that traffic to stay via using blogging. As a novice blogger, too, I learned the ropes on this the hard way. I continue to build out more and more content in addition to the books I self-publish (which I will touch on in this chapter, too but only briefly). The idea of writing a book would make almost everyone run away from this book quicker than quick so I will just discuss this in a high level way. If there is real interest in this, look for an updated Chapter on this in editions of this book moving forward.

Chapter 7 is the basics on structuring your business and identifying your mission or your mantra. This is the core idea of what you offer and your business idea. In Chapters 8, 9 and 10 we will be building your plan together. With insights, takeaways and space for you to add your own information, this book will become a draft of your business plan.

We will discuss managing for growth in Chapter 11. Chapter 12 will show you how to pull all of this information together into your official business documents and I want to hear from you in the feedback loop.

Be ready to go from zero to launch based off of my extensive experience as an entrepreneur since 2002 and my background in executing and teaching others to be entrepreneurial. I have spent countless classroom and seminar hours in rolling out my methods and plan on how to be an entrepreneur.

A huge part of this is what I discuss in the first book that really brings home the idea of how to be entrepreneurial; how to be risky in terms of aggressively measuring your worth, your skills and what you bring to the table. Do not make the mistake of discounting yourself in terms of who you are and what you can do. So many people limit themselves to the sidelines when they could be in the mainstream if they had the courage to try.

The first business I launched in 2002-2004 was focused on training and teaching other people and small businesses about how to train project managers and how to take the PMP exam and I can tell you firsthand about the ease of starting and running a profitable business NOW vs then.

The idea is that with technology and opportunity the way it is, you have to wonder why you have not launched already. I also run classes through Wagner College Department for Lifelong Learning on Entrepreneurship: Building your own business and this book will be used in conjunction with my course design and my first installment of this series.

This book is a professor's how to – I am the professor behind this book, this method and everything I espouse I have actually DONE in real life. I am not from the ivory tower; I have spent over 13 years in Corporate America, Higher Ed and as an entrepreneur, too. This book is actual time tested and because I have failed so many times, you can learn from me to avoid failure and go right for the success!

That being said, do not be afraid of failing. It is like when you are in school – if you fail it is how you know there is more for you to learn. You must think positively in terms of failure and learning to stay focused and on the path of entrepreneurship.

You will find yourself growing as a person and becoming a better career person, a better employee and with higher prospects by trying to be an entrepreneur. Also, with my techniques and my experience as your guide, you will avoid the common pitfalls that impact many other first time entrepreneurs.

If you have been an entrepreneur already, welcome! I am glad you found me so that you can be ready to execute and succeed this next time!!

Happy Hunting!

Chapter 1:

Business Ideas and On Execution

There are no dumb ideas. Same as in class there are no dumb questions. There are various ways to make a living in this new economy and for a lot of people, the traditional career path just does not exist anymore.

Finding one company to hire you and then staying with that company for 20, 30 or more years is a thing of the past (it is the recent past, though, because even when I was in Corporate America, I met many people who had worked 50 and even 60+ years at a company I was part of – and one such CEO rose from being a mailroom clerk to the CEO... So as recently as late 90's early 2000's, it was there, in person and not just corporate lore).

So to know if you have a business idea, you just have to think about what you love to do. Yes, it sounds hokey, but if you can do what you love and make money doing it, why would you do anything else?

What do you love to do?

I do not pretend to be a therapist – though I thought I wanted to be a psychologist many moons ago – you need to think about what you like to do. What do you like to do? Take a piece of paper and a pencil right now and write them down. Do you like to play video games? Why not consider blogging about games and current trends and seeing if that leads to potential income?

Do you like to make crafts? Look into Etsy and other local craft fairs and find out how to show your wares.

I will include some financial worksheets to use to make sense of your potential ideas (whatever they might be) to see if they really can make money because of course, with crafts or any other products, you do have the sunk cost of materials to move ahead with... even with intellectual products such as writing and /or consulting services, there is the cost of your time – you only have 24 hours in a day no matter who you are or what you are working on and at some point, you ended to see a return on any investment especially that of your time.

Writing Your Future Exercise

I did not invent this – it was created by a Professor who has used it to great success and it involves creating your narrative with your own words about what you want to achieve. I am sure it has been done in other ways and forms in other career counseling areas.

I was asked to do this as part of my last course for my MBA program in Rome. It was the final exam and it was meant to be a full booklet (or two) and it was about where we thought we would wind up in terms of careers.

It was interesting for me to write because at the time, I had no real work experience (other than a few internships and student worker and graduate assistant type work) but I was able to write more than two booklets about the career I envisioned for myself in financial services and in fact focused on an investment banking career.

I have used this technique many times in my career as entrepreneur, educator and executive. It helps that I love to write but even if you find writing to be a fate worse than death, you can still jot down quickly in bullet points or via your iPhone note app or whatever you use where you want to be in the future.

You can think more about the topics and ideas in the first book in this series on Entrepreneur-ING around what makes you happy and how you can find a way to monetize it.

I will tell you that it will not be easy but it will be worth it. If you can unlock your potential and look into running and creating something that is your own it can lead you to many other paths and career options.

The global economy has not grown enough to give anyone comfort in terms of their career growth. As we see an increase in robotics and artificial intelligence, the options for careers and how to grow one's career is tougher and tougher.

There is lots of competition out there and having the option for additional income or the protection (in theory) from being laid off and out of work for long stretches of time having a side-gig and/or an entrepreneurial pursuit can help you fill in the blank spaces on your resume OR give you something to explore and do for when you are not yet ready to retire.

I can say that 60 is the new 40 in terms of the ideals and pursuits of people. This is happening for many reasons – first of all, we must be taking better care of ourselves and our appearances than previous generations. When you have people delaying their childbearing years until their late 30's or 40's or beyond you see people less likely to retire. That means less jobs opening up for younger workers AND that sometimes "older" workers still want to work and launch their own businesses to help with this goal.

Spend some time thinking of what your future should entail/look like. Do not spend too long on this process though because you will find yourself paralysis by analysis.

There are tons of ideas and things you could work on but sometimes just starting is the hardest thing.

I have been entrepreneurial since 2002 but until I launched this business in 2015 and began using my words, my content and my image to promote it I was just spinning my wheels, so to speak. This is great because it means I have all of the expertise in failing so you can learn from my mistakes.

A big mistake is not keeping it simple. I could have launched in this same way over a decade ago. I mean we could argue that over a decade ago I had "less" to offer because I was just an educator for a few years and only working in corporate for a few, too.

So for you I would say to keep it simple – think about what you would like to see your future look like and how/if you can build a business around it. Think as though there are no limits. This is just an exercise to identify your options for your next steps.

As your professor, I do not want to leave this to chance. Right here I designed this fill in the blank write your own future exercise for you to use as a brainstorming tool. You can just take this and use it in one full paragraph as the future you want.

Write Your Future Fill in the Blanks:

In the future, I would like to be doing

_____

_____

_____

_____

_____

_____

_____

I would like to use/develop/build with these skills and talents

_____

_____

_____

_____

_____

_____

_____

My dream would be to make

_____ per month/quarter/year.

My clients would be

_____

_____

_____

_____

I would find my clients via

_____

_____

_____

_____

_____

_____

My business mission would be built around

_____

_____

_____

_____

_____

_____

_____

I would stand out in my marketplace because

_____

_____

_____

_____

_____

_____

_____

Interests & Vision Board

Something else that has been around for years and years is creating the idea of interests based vision board.

This can be as creative as you like. You can use photos, magazine photo spreads and more to represent this visual image of your future plan and what you want to do. Some of you can just use Pinterest for this but having it in person in front of you to hang on your wall and to use as inspiration is so much more powerful.

If you really cringe at art projects, you can skip this and just focus on the writing your future exercise; I will not fail you for this in fact I would understand you as someone who cringes when the glue comes out, too!

For those who create this, use the future exercise answers to pull together the look and feel of your future. As I said, this can be something you put on your wall and use it to motivate and inspire you as you move forward. I would love to see your vision boards so please send to me via Instagram @thenext_step123.

Chapter 2:

Business Plan Overview

There are tons of information about business plans on the internet and in books – but, this version of the business plan is based off of my 12+ years' experience as an entrepreneur AND 13+ years as an educator. This means you are getting the full "how do I do this" with the level of learning from someone who has actually done it in real life and failed and succeeded at it AND from someone who actually knows how to teach.

I have taught micro and macroeconomics for freshman in college and kept everyone awake; I have taught entrepreneurship to undergrads and graduate students all with the same focus on real world. As someone who knows how to teach and present information, this book is a unique opportunity to build out the information YOU need to go from zero to launch for your business.

The focus of this book is on building out the business plan that is actionable as well as being a living document. The plan will change and should be considered being written in "pencil" although most people will type their documents. It should be something that is reviewed again and again.

Here is the first business plan I ever wrote back in 2003-2004:

Business Tools 2 Go
Business Plan v1 Sole Proprietorship
Business License #

1.0 Executive Summary:

Business Tools 2 Go (BT2G) has been formed as a sole proprietorship owned and operated by Lisa A. Vento. This plan is written as a guide for starting and managing this new business and will also serve as the basis for a separate, detailed marketing plan. Following is a summary of the main points of this plan:

- ✓ Objectives of BT2G are to generate a profit, grow at a challenging and manageable rate, and to be a good citizen.
- ✓ Mission of BT2G is two fold – for college students and colleges and for small business owners. 1.) To provide undergraduate and graduate students at colleges and universities the tools and techniques of business, in one way by offering seminars to the universities in the New York City metropolitan area; 2.) Provide

project management expertise to small business owners.

- ✓ Keys to success for BT2G are marketing and networking, credentials and knowledge base of owner and generating repeat customers.
- ✓ Initial primary service will be hourly consulting; moving towards retainer contracts in future growth.
- ✓ Local market for this business is wide open for new and expanding consulting firms.
- ✓ Initial financial analysis of the viability of this venture shows outstanding promise and results. Several sources note that consulting business is easy to start, requires little up-front capital, and has the potential to be quite lucrative.

In conclusion, this plan projects rapid growth and high net profits over the next three years. Implementing this plan, in conjunction with a comprehensive and detailed marketing plan, will ensure that BT2G rapidly becomes a profitable venture for the owner.

1.1 Objectives

The objectives of this business plan are:

1. To provide a written guide for starting and managing this consulting business; a strategic framework for developing a comprehensive tactical marketing plan.

2. The intended audience is the owner of this business only; this plan is not intended to obtain financing from outside sources.
3. The scope of this plan is to provide detailed monthly projections for the current plan year and yearly summaries for the next two years.

The objectives of BT2G are:

1. Profit – to generate sufficient profit to finance future growth and to provide the resources needed to achieve the other objectives of the company and its owner. Net profit of 65% of sales in the first year.
2. Growth – to grow the business at a rate that is both challenging and manageable, leading the market with innovation and adaptability. (Grow from 10 hours per week to 35 hours per week.)
3. Citizenship – to be an intellectual and social asset to the community and environment. (Contribute 5 hours per week as a volunteer, contribute 5% of pretax profits to charity).

1.2 Mission

BT2G's mission is simple and straightforward:

✓ Purpose: BT2G exists to provide fast, reliable technical assistance to small businesses and undergraduate/graduate students. BT2G sells tools & techniques!

- ✓ Vision: By providing fast response, informed expertise, and consistently high quality solutions, BT2G generates enough satisfied repeat customers to provide a stable retainer base. This generates sufficient profit to provide a comfortable living for the owner.
- ✓ Mission: The short-term objective is to start this company quickly and inexpensively, with a minimum of debt. The long-term objective is to grow the company into a stable and profitable entity that the owner can easily and comfortably manage.
- ✓ Marketing Slogan: "Business Tools 2 Go is your one stop source for transitioning from Classroom to Boardroom." "Business Tools 2 Go for your small business' Project Management needs!"

1.3 Keys to Success

Keys to Success for BT2G are:

- ✓ Marketing and Networking
- ✓ Responsiveness
- ✓ Quality
- ✓ Tools & Techniques
- ✓ Relationship Building

2.0 Company Description:

Business Tools 2 Go (a/k/a BusinessTools2Go.com; BT2G) will be a start-up venture with the following characteristics:

- ✓ BT2G will be a sole proprietorship, initially.
- ✓ Goal is to start the venture as inexpensively as possible, with no debt financing.
- ✓ Operations will be run out of a home-office start up.

2.1 Company Ownership:

BT2G will be created initially as a sole proprietorship, owned and operated by Lisa A. Vento. Incorporation, probably as a LLC, will be explored as a later option.

2.2 Start-up Summary:

As a home-based consulting business, start-up costs are very low. Initial investment was in the owner, Lisa A. Vento's MBA degree, which was received in

July of 1999 from the Rome, Italy campus of St. John's University.

Additional expenses include minor miscellaneous, including $120.00 to register the business with the county clerk's office in Staten Island.

Start-up	

Requirements	

Start-up Expenses	
License	$120
Stationery etc.	$100
Brochures	$125
Web site URL and development	$120
Total Start-up Expenses	$465

Start-up Assets Needed	
Cash Balance on Starting Date	$35
Other Current Assets	$0
Total Current Assets	$35

Long-term Assets	$0
Total Assets	$35

Investment	
Owner Investment	$500.00
Other	$0
Total Investment	$500.00

Current Liabilities	
Accounts Payable	$0
Current Borrowing	$0
Other Current Liabilities	$0

Current Liabilities	$0

Long-term Liabilities	$0
Total Liabilities	$0

Loss at Start-up	($465)
Total Capital	$35
Total Capital and Liabilities	$35

2.3 Company Locations and Facilities

This is a home office venture.

- ✓ Computer facilities initially consist of the owner's existing system.
- ✓ Telephone – one line currently serves the location; data connection via cable modem.
- ✓ Utilities are included in rent of home.

3.0 Services

BT2G offers consulting services to three primary markets: Undergraduate/Graduate Students, Universities and Small Business Owners.

For Undergraduate/Graduate Students, BT2G will offer one-stop shopping for the following:

- ✓ Resume Writing
- ✓ Presentation Skills
- ✓ Interviewing Skills
- ✓ How to Network to a Career
- ✓ Other Career search techniques and methodologies
- ✓ Research/Paper Writing skills

For Universities, BT2G will offer Seminars on:

- ✓ Networking
- ✓ Interviewing Skills
- ✓ Resume Writing
- ✓ Presentation Skills

For Small Business Owners, BT2G will offer:

- ✓ Project Management Expertise in:
  - o Feasibility Studies
  - o Project Plans
  - o Quality Assurance

- ✓ Specifications/Technical Writing
- ✓ Web Site Design/HTML Coding
- ✓ Training on
    - ○ Negotiation Skills

Detailed descriptions of these points are found in the sections below.

3.1 Service Description

BT2G will offer two main billing types, corresponding to what industry experts have identified as the primary opportunities in consulting:

1. **Hourly** - The less traditional sort of short term assignment helping a client with a resume, interviewing skills, etc. Also included in this would be seminar fees for Universities.
2. **Retainer** - For small businesses, highlighting owner's particular area of expertise of Project Management.

3.2 Competitive Comparison

There seems to be minor amounts of competition in the county of Richmond for the depth and breadth of services offered by BT2G. There are a few resume-writing facilities located in New Dorp but very few full-service shops like BT2G.

3.3 Sales Literature

BT2G will start with basic literature to establish market position.

- ✓ Logo and Theme: Logo will include a miniature tool box, in keeping with the company name.
- ✓ Stationary & Business Cards: Will be purchased via SIC Printing on Buel Avenue in Staten Island.
- ✓ Brochure: Will be done in-house along with Flyers for positioning at major universities.
- ✓ Advertising: Done via Chamber of Commerce in Richmond, SI; various school papers at universities in Staten Island and via Victory Bank flyer.
- ✓ Web Presence: A Web site is under development, with the URL www.businesstools2go.com. This Web site should launch shortly.

3.4 Fulfillment

The fulfillment of services for BT2G is provided by the owner. The ultimate deliverable is the owner's expertise and problem solving ability, coupled with an open mind and ease of communication that will result in the customer's complete confidence in immediate and lasting results.

4.0 Market Analysis:

BT2G services will be brought by:
- ✓ Universities
- ✓ Undergraduate/Graduate Students
- ✓ Small Business Owners

Student and University clients would prefer to deal with BT2G because of the sole proprietorship owner's expertise and knowledge of the job markets, techniques and tools that can be taught and instilled to assist their transition from the classroom to the boardroom.

Small business owners would prefer to deal with BT2G because of the extensive tools, techniques and experience in project management, specification writing and business plans of the owner.

5.0Marketing Strategy:

BT2G will focus on the following to establish and grow the business:

- ✓ Four main promotion strategies: networking and referrals, web-based promotions, traditional media advertising and some non-traditional promotion methods.
- ✓ A value proposition of timely and practical tools & techniques, at a reasonable rate.
- ✓ A competitive edge based on cultivating existing customer relationships.
- ✓ A comprehensive and detailed marketing and sales strategy, covered in depth in a separate marketing plan.

5.1Strategy Pyramids

- ✓ Strategy 1 – Networking & Referrals – using existing contacts and clients to build a larger network of potential clients.
- ✓ Strategy 2 – Web Promotion – using a Web page to showcase the owner's skills and knowledge, providing an "electronic brochure" as well as useful information.
- ✓ Strategy 3 – Advertising – Traditional methods such as newspaper ads.

✓ Strategy 4 – Non-Traditional – Creative and unique advertising such as door hangers, bumper stickers, etc.

A much more comprehensive discussion of these strategies is presented in the BT2G Marketing Plan.

5.2 Value Proposition

The value proposition offered by BT2G is simple: timely and practical tools & techniques for students making the transition to their first career and small businesses project management needs.

5.3 Competitive Edge

BT2G's competitive edge is that the owner already has a significant number of high quality relationships with current and potential clients.

5.4 Marketing Strategy

The topics below briefly outline the marketing strategy for BT2G. A much more comprehensive discussion of these strategies is presented in Marketing Plan.

5.4.1 Positioning Statement

BT2G offers timely and practical tools & techniques for students making the transition to their first career and small businesses project management needs.

5.4.2 Pricing Strategy

BT2G will adopt the following pricing strategy:

For Students:

Hourly Rate: $40.00 per hour

For Universities:

Seminar/Public Speaking: $1,000 per session

For Small Businesses:

Hourly Rate: $100.00 per hour

5.4.3 Promotion Strategy

The primary promotion strategy for BT2G will be directly in line with strategy pyramids mentioned previously. The lead strategy will be to focus on cultivating existing relationships, using known networking techniques to develop referrals and new customer leads. Added to this will be a blend of web based marketing and traditional public relations and media marketing. The ultimate promotion strategy, however, will be in guaranteeing customer satisfaction: happy customers will generate repeat and new business.

5.4.4 Marketing Programs

The most important marketing program for BT2G is to get the word out, through a combination of the following:

- ✓ Sending a letter of announcement and brochure to all existing contacts and customers.
- ✓ Following the well-established steps of a public relations campaign (press releases, announcements, etc.).
- ✓ Developing and purchasing, "Grand Opening" announcements in local news media.

A much more comprehensive discussion of these programs is presented in Marketing Plan.

5.5 Sales Strategy

Sales strategy for BT2G is simple and straightforward: Customer Satisfaction! Happy customers will be repeat customers and will provide referrals.

A much more comprehensive discussion of the sales strategy is presented in the Marketing Plan.

5.5.1 Sales Forecast

TBD

5.6 Strategic Alliances

BT2G will need to focus on networking with local universities, small businesses and other organizations (such as Chamber of Commerce) to develop strategic alliances. Such organizations, even if not customers themselves, will be valuable in providing leads to new customers.

My current business plan looks very different but I am not ready to share it because I feel it contains too much proprietary information but that might for future editions of this book.

We will be over the course of future chapters be breaking up the business plan as I know it to be best for you to use and personalize as needed.

I also will be available in terms of sharing ideas and best processes – this book will be updated as more happens in the industry and I am using it as a base "textbook" for my courses on entrepreneurship and I do encourage you to reach out to me via social media or my website to share with me your results of applying my lessons from this book.

Remember, I have been an entrepreneur since 2004 and I have already made some mistakes and had some failures which means that by learning with me and my books, you can avoid the mistakes I have already made and learn best practices from someone who has actually done these things in their real life.

Chapter 3

On Websites

I have written extensively on my blog and shared via social media that starting an online business today is one of the easiest things to do.

When I began my first company in 2004, there was no integrated payment system via the website development services I could afford. You needed to hire a bank to be the processer of credit card payments and you could not incorporate texting or chat functions in your site.

Plus, without social media, the only way to drive people to your website was to pay tons of money to Google Adwords (trust me –at the time I paid almost $600 and got nothing out of it at all) or to place print advertisements around to get people to go to your website. There were no smart phones as we know them today or social media as we know it today. There was no low-cost strategy to get your name out there.

It was the same uphill battle in 2005-2007 when my husband and I owned a retail store – the only way to promote our location and products was through expensive print ads and although we had a website, no one could be driven to it without spending hard earned money to promote it.

Now, I use social media exclusively and I get between 300-600 people a DAY on my site. Yes a day. I do use other important pieces in my strategy – I create content 5 days a week through my blog and share it across different social media accounts. I will talk more about these topics in Chapter 4 and 6.

The best way to begin any company today is to have a website. Well, I should say the only way to have a company today is to have a website. If you do not have a website, you have a credibility issue. Not only do you need a website, but it also needs to be attractive and include some multi-media content.

You do not need to be a computer person to have a website today. There are many different service providers that have templates that you can personalize using rudimentary technological knowledge or you can look into hiring an expert to help you build out your website. For instance, I recently launched small business services that include website advisement and turnkey blogging functionality.

I am writing this chapter about what I know best. I have in the past used register.com and although that service worked ok for me in the past it was too long ago for me to discuss. Features and functionality changes so quickly.

Weebly.com is a simple, easy to use and intuitive web building site. You can, without any web knowledge, be able to create and launch a website like TODAY.

You can launch that website for free at first so long as you do not mind having the word "weebly" in your URL. So when I first launched my website, the URL is www.thenextstep1234.weebly.com and to remove the "weebly", I had to pay a certain amount to upgrade to a more professional site.

No matter what line of business you are interested in launching, you need a website. Even if you do not plan on ever having a storefront (which most do not have today), you still need a "store" available on the internet. It is so important to have this presence. The minute you share your business name, someone will ask you for the web address or search for you on Google. If they do not find a website, they will forget about you.

Even worse, if they find a website and it looks unprofessional or like it was designed and launched in 1994 – well it will count against you, too.

In building your website, you should start with templates that are already designed and available via your web hosting company. If you have expertise in coding or design, then by all means create your own design template.

Choose your colors to represent your company and you can change the hues of any pre-designed template. Make sure you use photos that are representative of your company and you. Use placeholders for the interim but as you build out your business, personalize the headers and other areas of your webpage with your images.

This takes time, though and you can begin small. Start with a main page and your contact information and of course with a blog page which will discuss in more detail later in the book.

You can use your website extensively in your marketing plan. After all, creating and sharing content can be a great way to promote your business and your services.

I would be remiss if I did not mention that my company offers turnkey operations for blogging and website development for small businesses and you can find out more about this service at www.thenextstep1234.com.

That website you create should represent you – as authentic as possible and you can link it to your LinkedIn profile and use it as a base for your Twitter and Instagram posts, all of which we will address more later.

Emulate companies in your industry or niche and see what works for you and what does not. If you can create a logo, do so. There are free websites out there that can create a logo based off of some of your information and you should check it out.

With website design, you can also consider your business card design and set up so that there is some uniformity that flows through to your brand and creation of your company.

You should be thinking of your company as a brand from day one. Think about how you want to present your brand and what should be the reminder of what your company is and how it stands out in the marketplace.

The most important thing is to have a great looking "landing" or home page. Try to keep it professional and uncluttered. As time goes on, you can build out more content and pages to your site. I find sometimes that I have too many pages because of have each of my product lines and my books and my speaking engagements, and well you get the idea.

In building your website, one of the most important things to include is a blog. I will be talking more about blogging in Chapter 6 but it should be the cornerstone of your website and your branding, marketing plans, too.

It helps to know some HTML coding but it is not necessary. Most of the website creation software is built around do it yourself without coding knowledge.

There are different pricing plans for when you need to build out the website to look more professional. You should pick your color schemes around what looks pleasing to you and what looks pleasing on the eyes.

Also, you should use your Instagram marketing for use on your website design, too. This can seem overwhelming and if you think too hard about it, you might not move forward. It is important to jump forward and go for it – as you build out your content, you can then more personalize and create your brand with the website.

As I said, the most important thing is to create a website period – end of story. You have to create it in order to be legitimate and to share your business with the world. Yes, I said world. There are no barriers anymore to business and commerce. If you build it, they will come (yes, that was a cheesy Field of Dreams quote – but it is true).

You have to think big in the back of your mind. I see web traffic from around the world on my website because the world is truly flat. Having a website and following my plan for marketing via blogging and social media can help you do the same, too.

Of the 1500-2000+ people per week that are on my site, some of them buy from me and others partner with me and create new opportunities that I never would have thought of on my own. The original business plan I had for The Next Step was focused on resumes, cover letters, application essays and resumes for colleges.

The plan has expanded to include robust workshops, online learning centers and teleseminars around college, career readiness and small business blogging and website development. It is amazing how much things grow and change when you put it out into the world via your website and marketing plan.

The shopping experience for your site should be seamless – once you begin offering your services or products via the site, you MUST upgrade to a paid site and this is true for any provider. You can use PayPal or other servicing to process payments. You can also consider using SQUARE for when you are out at events and make a sale on site.

I look forward to hearing how you do this – if you try Weebly and move ahead with it, send me the link and I will share it with my network! Create and maintain that feedback loop with me as you build out your business, website, plan and more with my lessons – I am your professor, after all!

Chapter 4:

What is Marketing?

As someone who studied marketing for my BS degree but never officially "worked" in marketing as my corporate career was more focused around financial services, publishing and in roles as project management / technology guru running my own businesses has been the marketing nirvana for me.

I talk a lot in my workshops, training and classes about technology and how the advents in this field has made it easy for anyone to open a business and to be found and successful with said business.

There is so much available out there today that just did not exist 5 or 10 years ago. When I first launched my business in 2004, there was no social media. There were no ability to create and process payments without partnering with a banking service provider to do it. Well, you get the idea of what there was not in existence.

Marketing is all about getting the name of your business and the services/products you provide out there. The trick of marketing is to do it as cheaply (or as free) as possible. For me, my marketing budget is as close to zero as possible and I will share the way you can market your business for as close to $0 as possible, too!

The point of this book is to get you to go from zero to launch as quickly as possible – not having access to a ton of capital should NOT be a reason to miss the chance to be your own boss.

In the world today, the economy is such that having a side gig might wind up being your only gig – there is not much opportunity available as people looking for opportunity and learning how to create your own opportunity is key to making it in this new economy.

Marketing is all about the 5 P's – place, product, price, promotion, and PROFIT.

Place

The components are all built according to what you are doing but for most of us, the placement is virtual. At least, for me it is (aside from my books as those are physical goods), everything I provide and do as a business is virtually stored in my intellect, with my work on resumes and branding packages and my workshops, training and seminars. It is all a service based just in time delivery system.

Product

This is literally whatever it is you are interested in selling or providing. Is it a thing – what is it? Maybe art or a gadget or maybe you are considering importing something to sell or exporting something – perhaps you are considering buying a franchise. This product is the basis of the business. Maybe you are the product – you are a consultant and you provide services around business creation or something similar to what I do with helping people take their next steps. Whatever it is that you do, consider how you create it, what you name it, etc. It is your product and it should stand out as being from your company.

Do not be afraid to add and remove products, as needed. Do not remove something that is a top seller, though unless you really need to. Beware of product liability laws and how what you are selling is regulated. This could take up 20 books so know where to look for what you need or rely on my as a consultant/expert – create that feedback loop and ask me to connect you with the resources you need or go to your trust Google.com.

Anything you need to know can be researched and looked into from your computer. You should know this information and we will talk more about it in the appropriate business plan section further in the book.

Price

You need to identify your price and be careful with it – if you price too low, people will think you are not worth it. If you price too high, people will think you are not worth it. It is challenging and I have already adjusted my prices many times in this journey with The Next Step. I began with low low pricing and found it did not meet the value of what I was offering. I have now adjusted my prices accordingly and believe it or not, I get MORE sales now than ever even though my pricing went from $25 a resume to $200+ per resume.

It is all about the value and the excellent service you provide. For me, I know I am the best at improving people's resumes. The best – I have been doing this for 15+ years and I can take someone's flat file and make it shine and get them opportunities they otherwise would have missed out on or been overlooked because their resume and other documents did not reflect how awesome they are in real life.

Work on your pricing - check out your competition (we will talk more about this in market research chapter) but know what they are charging and compare who you are and what you bring to the field accordingly.

Know that pricing is a work in progress and understand that you can and should adjust accordingly, as needed.

Promotion

Promotion is everything – it is what you need to do to get your name and your company out there. It is the way you will create and lead to profit for your firm.

Promotion does not have to cost money. It can cost money, though. I would suggest that if you have the money to invest in promotion via media ads, placements and/or radio spots then by all means, do so. I will say that you do not NEED to do this, though. I mean, it can help but it is not necessary.

What is necessary is identifying and building on your niche. What it is that you want to be known for and how you can share that message across the world or your town so that you can build your business? Promotion is about making sure potential customers know you exist and know how to find you.

When you built a website in the early 2000's (before social media), you would have to then advertise that URL in the newspapers and trust someone would then go and type it in to a web browser and any online advertising you did was spotty and/or super expensive and/or not going to get your any results.

Now, with social media and great content, you can be known and found by anyone who might be a customer or you can be found by tons of people who would never hire you but maybe know someone who would hire you. In my mind, if you do the promotion as close to cheaply as possible and even if you overshoot your intended audience, this is ok. You can then as you make money with your business budget some of it towards future marketing efforts that are more targeted to just whom you want to get noticed by in the world.

For now, though, you are new and everyone and their mother should know about you. Start with your network and promote yourself as much as you can. I use my personal Facebook account and my friends and family to share the word.

I always talk about how hard it is for me to promote my business to this group as I feel embarrassed or I do not want them to think I am "using" them to get business but I learned really quickly that without promoting to my friends and family I am doing my business and my relationships a disservice. Everyone who knows and loves you wants to do well and those that secretly hate you will be interested in watching you fail so win – win as it gets more people to your site and sharing your content. Even if it is just to hate read it ...

Profit

This is the goal, of course. The ability for your own business to make a profit. Profit meaning after all of the expenses and costs to produce, launch and promote is a positive number.

As someone who has been an entrepreneur for the past 12+ years, I know that profit can be very hard to achieve. It can be near impossible. But that does not mean you should not try.

I think that 12 years ago it was even harder to be profitable because no one would know you existed. Now, with hard work and determination, I think almost anyone can identify their niche, create a business and make money with it if they are willing to work really hard and stay focused on the long term plan. With me as your guide, you will succeed and you then can keep me informed of all the great things you are doing with your business!

Chapter 5:

Social Media Savvy

Social media must become your favorite thing in the whole world. I have written countless social media exposes and my secrets of social media for my blog. I am going to create new rules here and share even MORE than I ever did on my blog – this is all new and all for you, my fellow entrepreneur so that you can harness the power of social media! OK, I am done sounding like a self-help book now...

If you had told me before I launched The Next Step in July 2015 that I would use Twitter, Instagram and have my own YOUTUBE channel I would have told you that you were insane.

I am an "old" meaning I am not digitally native and although I had a Twitter account, I never ever used it and I did not understand it. At all.

I now use Twitter – and have over 4000 followers (follow me @thenext_step123) and Instagram is something I love to do with creating photos and collages that document my journey as an entrepreneur and shares my lessons and more (also @thenext_step123). My YouTube channel has over 100 videos (and counting) and I create and share so much on that channel regarding my business, my products and my failures, too.

Here is your blueprint so to speak on social media – what to do and how in general terms.

<u>Twitter & Instagram</u>

I am putting these two tools together because they integrate super well. You can share to both from Instagram and your Twitter benefits from sharing those longer form posts.

You should create profiles for your business or yourself as the business owner. This can be tricky if you are also a professional who is juggling a side gig. Keep in mind that you have to be careful if you work for a corporation that does not approve of side gigs or if you need to spend time creating your business on company time.

Know your rules for the company where you work if you are going to build a side gig. You do not want anyone else making the decision for you to leap into only entrepreneurship – it has to be your choice.

For your Twitter and Instagram strategy, we will take Twitter first and then discuss Instagram.

Twitter

Your use of Twitter can be done under the company name but it would be best if you can also brand it with your information. If you have another job and this is not possible, then go for the company brand only.

You can start slow with Twitter. Once you set up your account and decide how you will brand it either just your company or you and your company, it depends on your choice.

You should begin by following things in your field and/or industry. Follow some of your competition to see what they do and how they do it. If something applies to what you are selling or offering as a service, then share it by retweeting it – you can install Twitter on your smartphone or use it from your desktop.

To fully run the social media of your business, you really need to have the app(s) on your phone. If you also have a personal account or some other account, be careful not to mix them up.

When something applies to you or your offerings, you can retweet it and include reference to your website and/or what you are doing in general. When you set up your account, you really need to include your company website address in your profile and make sure you can retweet things that apply to you and include your web address, too.

Use bit.ly to shorten the URLs, as needed. With only 140 characters, you definitely need to be careful with the length of your postings. When you are ready and dependent on your blogging routine (see Chapter 6), it will be time to use a service to manage the tweeting.

I use SocialOomph and for $12/month, I have the ability to use photos and text or just text and can schedule it to run as I want to either every two hours or every 12 hours.

There are other tools to use to automate social media and you can check them out but I know from my experience that SocialOomph works for what I need it to do. You can program a message to send out to anyone who follows you and you can chose to auto follow back anyone who follows you.

I liken Twitter to yelling in a room – sometimes it feels like "no one" is looking at your tweets but eventually, with the right use of the dreaded hashtags, you can gain some real traction. I began tweeting in July and I started with zero followers and now I have over 4100 followers. I use CrowdFire app to know who unfollows me so that I can unfollow back. It really is a math issue – there is a ratio of followers to followees so at some point, you get the max number of people you can follow and then you need to unfollow someone to follow someone else.

I find a lot of website traffic comes from my Twitter content and I "meet" new people and gain new followers all of the time. Be careful with Twitter as anything you post is in real time and even if you make a mistake and delete it, someone might have snapped a picture of it and as you know with social media and the internet mistakes are often made and these mistakes can lead to you going viral in a bad way.

Instagram

With Instagram, I am much newer to this tool as I only started my Instagram account in late October 2015. I am at almost 600 followers but I do find that tons of people like and comment on my photos and some of them follow only. That being said, it is another way to promote my business and what I do. I create photo collages using the free Layout app to create real images that represent being an entrepreneur and what I do. I find this to be an amazing tool. I can use and reuse the photos on my blog, my website and my tweets, too.

I do not use a service to schedule my "grams" or my Instagram posts. I do this in the moment. That being said, sometimes I take a picture or collage and use it in my SocialOomph to share the picture with a tweet over and over or just one time, depending on the content. Because I now have over 200+ blog posts, I have tons of content being shared and retweeted and shared again so I love using these tools to share more.

I also recommend another free app Instaquote that can allow you to create your own words in a photo like feature so almost like a meme or something that looks really cool. You can make the background one of your pictures or use the free designs available; you can then save the photo to your cell phone photo roll and use it in

Layout to create a collage or you can Instagram it directly as a stand-alone photo.

The best thing about Instagram is there is no 140 character limit. You can still use hashtags but you can tell more of a story in this format.

People can find your Instagram by your hashtags, too, just like with Twitter.

Using these tools together can provide your clients and soon to be clients with a real insider's view into what you do and what you can do for them. Be cautious with what you post.

Both Twitter and Instagram offer ad programs where you can promote your tweet or create an Instagram ad. I have created Twitter ads in the past and did spend a couple of hundred dollars on that but found ultimately that my own grassroots marketing efforts were just as effective, if not more so, than paying for the ads.

I have never tried to create an Instagram ad; with only 590 or so followers since end of October, maybe I would think about it but it seems people follow and unfollow quite quickly on Instagram so it might not be worth it as lots of people react to your pictures and obviously are getting your message even if they do not follow you.

Facebook

You should create a Facebook page for your business but beware that Facebook is becoming an "older" app and it can be tough to gain traction on Facebook without paying for advertising or "promote my page" ads.

I did do this at one point and spent some money promoting my page – it did get results but I do not want to consistently pay for something that I might be able to achieve through my content. I do find Facebook to be the one field of social media marketing where I have struggled to make a dent without paying money.

I continue to link my Twitter with my Facebook account so that my tweets are on my business page. I do also post things on the fly to my Facebook page to make it more dynamic and run specials and other coupon type things on Facebook to make it grow. I however still hover around 200+ likes only.

If you find a Facebook strategy that works, please share it with me! As a professor, I find I often learn the most from my students so teach me!

YouTube

YouTube is so much fun for me and it is a learning process. You need lighting, good audio and a story to tell. I have over 100 videos and some of them are awesome – others are not too great. However, I keep them and show it as my learning curve and equipment changes.

I do not pay to promote these videos and I do not allow YouTube to run ads on my videos, either. I am only creating and sharing these videos to share my message and I do not want people to shy away from watching them.

I have 8 subscribers right now – I do not know how much of an impact YouTube will have for me but over 500+ views of my videos and I integrate the videos into my site and my blog posts.

I found a free app called "KnowMe" which I highly recommend for you to use with your YouTube channel. From your smartphone, you can create 3-minute movies using photos in the background and also other media clips. It is a way to be a movie director on a small scale.

You can create your story, your narrative and it automatically can be shared via Facebook and Twitter. Also, you can then take the video on your cell phone and put it directly to your YouTube channel.

Can you believe the ways in which you can run a business directly from your phone? You can be creating videos for YouTube in your car like I do (the lighting is fabulous) and obviously I do not do this while driving.

I also use my computer with a program called Camtasia to create a record my screen along with video of me "teaching" for certain things.

Another program I use is VoiceThread which is about $20/month and allows me to use PowerPoints of my own creation and then overlay video and audio and written notes to the content slide by slide.

All of this content I create can be shared via YouTube or my blog directly.

LinkedIn

This is tricky for those of you who have an alternate career. If your entrepreneurship route is your main source of employment, you can use that on your LinkedIn profile. You can include links to your website and other information. Also, SocialOomph does link with LinkedIn so you can schedule posts.

I would not post the same stuff over and over on LinkedIn, though, because it is more flat meaning people will visit your page and see it replicated. Instead, share things once a day if you blog. If you do not blog, focus on sharing content and news from your industry along with exciting things about your business, as you can.

SnapChat

I just started using SnapChat; I cannot speak much to this but I do know it is used by all of the younger people. I create snaps and share them to MyStory and NYStory which keeps it "live" for 2 days or so and people can view it but again, I am so new to SnapChat I think a future installment of this book will talk more about how to do this.

Teleseminars & Moodle (online learning center)

I am using InstantTeleseminar to create lessons based content with audio lessons for people to dial into or to record it and reuse it for other ways.

Also, I have a Moodle online classroom for training and more. If you are interested in these two types of content creation, follow up with me directly as these are specifically for people who are offering types of services that involve consulting and/or presenting.

Anything you do on web based products or with social media can be shared and used to build your brand. One of the most important things you can do and share is your own content, created through a blog. More on that in Chapter 6.

Chapter 6:

Blogging

Why is blogging important? Blogging is key to running a business end of story. You can use social media like a champ but without sharing your own thoughts and words in longer format, you cannot stand out from the crowd.

I spend $0 on marketing but I get between 1500-2000 people a week on my website (sometimes, I get even more than 2000). Some of those people hire me for their next step but even if they do not hire me, they are learning with me and potentially coming back to me in the future and hiring me then.

I build my credibility with my blog. When I started blogging in July I relied on other articles and just posted my thoughts around those other articles. By September, I was creating my own articles, my own content and these are not short articles by any means. I have written on how to interview, how to write a college application essay and more. I create short videos to go with my blog posts and integrate them together. I share the content I create via Facebook, LinkedIn, Twitter and Instagram, too.

I found I had so much to say that I have written and published 3 books of 20k words each (give or take) – this book will be my 4th published book once it is done.

The content I create and write for my books is totally different than what is on my blog. The idea or the topic might germinate in my blog but what I do with the books is totally new and original. In other words, I do not copy and paste from my blog to my books.

This book is exciting because even though it is my 4th book, it is the one I am most destined to write with all of my experience in running businesses. I teach entrepreneurship both as a professor for college students and through a partnership with Wagner College Department for Lifelong Learning for adults looking to continue their careers or start something new.

If you can write and live to write like I do then consider building off your blogging with your own books. There is nothing like walking into a meeting or pitching your company and referencing your books that you wrote.

For the blog though, with Weebly, I can "tag" my posts to categories. I have a ton of categories and then I can create social media posts tying into categories to showcase my skills and why someone should hire me. It works.

If you hate writing, consider outsourcing your blogging. For instance, I charge $500 to create and launch a small business website with blog then a monthly maintenance fee, depending on how often the blogging schedule is going to be and what the blog should be about.

What is more important than having someone else managing your blog though is finding your voice. You really need a way to "connect" with your customers, potential customers and your audience. There are some people who will just promote you and/or read your content and enjoy it so much that they will come back again and again – this is good; these are your "people" they get your message and they share it.

Some visitors to your site will be enthralled and contact you or actually hire you directly (or buy from you). It is important to have a reason to get people to your site. You should not just post over and over again all over social media that "Hi, I have a business – buy from me!" I mean you can do that a few times but not all the time.

Instead, by using a blog, you can identify and share things about your business or thoughts on your industry or anything to establish yourself as an expert or as someone who should be followed.

The blogging really is the crux of the social media and marketing plan. I understand if you are shy and not sure of why or how to do this but I will tell you that to get your business to succeed you really need to consider blogging. There is no reason for you or anyone really to follow my schedule (5 days a week except major holidays) or my length of posts (all over 500 + words some even more) – I mean, I did write 3+ books of 20k words each so obviously I love to write. Instead, make a schedule that works for you and stick to what you know. Organize your content.

My routine is that on a weekend, I spend time organizing my blog post ideas. I take an hour to do this, tops. I brainstorm on what I want to write about, keeping in mind what I have already written or checking to make sure I did not cover it already.

Then I try to draft out as much of my posts as I can during the weekend so that I can just format and post them into my Website with whatever pictures or media I want to include.

Sometimes, I do more of this on the weekend and sometimes I scramble for a post at the last minute. I try never to miss a day although some of my mentors have said I could change my frequency or adjust my length as it does take me some time to compile and create this content.

I find blogging helps me organize my thoughts and even inspires new product offerings and new book ideas. I use the blog to plan out new events, new ideas and more. I then also use the blog posts to build out recognition and interest in my company. I plug in many links to other content I created and even to my products and services. I promote my books, myself and my business exclusively on my blog.

Recently, I was asked to contribute articles to another website about books called NFReads.com, which I did and I am also a guest blogger for Teachers.org, coming soon.

Being able to write and weave a story is huge. If you truly hate writing, consider creating a VLOG instead of a Blog – this is all video based and you can integrate just the videos to your website instead of your written word.

The best way for you to learn how to blog is to read other blogs in your field or interest and see what they do and how. I know for a fact I am quite prolific and much more prolific than anyone else in my field. I do sense the day coming when I will have to cut back on my writing but even still with all of the new business, clients and partnerships I am working on, I always find time to create a quick blog post to share where I am or something I learned whether it is something I learned recently or 10+ years ago – I share it as it flows.

I also focus on writing my books and also write my own Press Releases, too. If you would like to learn more, check out my blog and learn with me as I go!

Chapter 7:

Mission Statements & Structure

Your mission statement is key. It is so important and should be quick and to the point. This does not need to be a million words. It should be succinct and yours.

Here is my mission:

The Next Step is built around college and career readiness. My experience as an educator and an executive helps new graduates, high school students and career professionals to take their next steps in both their career and education goals. I create content and offer interactive and informative seminars on college and career readiness, entrepreneurship and more.

I work one-on-one with clients to help them with their resumes, cover letters, LinkedIn Profiles and application essays. As part of my service, I include coaching and career plans without additional costs. I am interested in speaking at your event in the NYC / Staten Island area on any of the topics included in my blog.

I also created an Instaquote about it:

What is The Next Step?

The Next Step is built around college and career readiness. My experience as an educator and an executive helps new graduates, high school students and career professionals take their next steps to career and education goals.

I create content and offer interactive and informative seminars on college and career readiness, entrepreneurship, and more.

Also, I work one-on-one with clients to help them with resumes, cover letters, LinkedIn profiles and application essays. As part of my service, I include coaching and career plans without extra cost.

I am interested in speaking at your event to teach how to be ready for the next step.

Lisa Vento Nielsen, more at
www.thenextstep1234.com

I use that photo in my social media marketing on both Twitter, Instagram and my website, too.

Your mission should be as succinct and complex as possible. It should highlight what you do and how you do it.

You can create and recreate it, as needed and as your business changes based on client taste or input. You should have it be clear and simple.

Draft something below on what you would want to see in your mission statement. It should include what you do, how you do it and why you do it.

Draft Mission Statement

_____

_____

_____

_____

_____

_____

_____

_____

_____

Business Structure

This is something I cover over and over again in classes such as Corporate Finance and Entrepreneurship, too. There are many types of business structure and you should choose what best fits your needs or what is important for your industry.

For instance, if you sell a dietary supplement that you invented, you maybe want to be a corporation so that just in case, you can protect your personal assets in the event of disaster with your product.

If you have a retail store location and people are coming in and out, you really need special insurance in case someone gets hurt in your store and you should be a corporation to protect your personal assets, too.

The options for business ownership are: sole proprietorship, partnership, corporation and Limited Liability Company. Before choosing your business structure, you should consult with your network, accountant and lawyer to be sure you are using the right structure to benefit your business and protect your personal assets, as needed.

Sole Proprietorship

The easiest type of business type to begin but also the least protected, so to speak. If you are a sole proprietor, the business lives and dies with you. You are the business; it comes through your own personal tax returns by filling a Schedule C (see an accountant for more on this).

You will need a sole proprietorship EIN number (Employer Identification Number) – even if you do not have any employees. This will allow you to have a separate id for the business instead of using your Social Security Number for the business.

In addition, to create a business bank account, you need to file for a business license or a DBA from the town/city in which you are operating your business. With those two pieces of information, you can get your business bank account and keep your business income separate from your personal accounts.

Partnership

If you are going into business with another person(s), you can create a partnership. This is something you should consider meeting with a lawyer for or creating a legal document via the internet that can specify who owns what, who has what role/task and what decisions could be makes by whom. It can also specify what assets are brought to the business and what would happen if the business were to be dissolved or if only one wants to dissolve or if there is an interest in selling the business to just one of the partners.

There is also a limited liability partnership which would also have to be set up legally to limit the losses to the investments of the partners.

Again, meeting with an accountant and/or lawyer is helpful and advised.

Corporation

Corporate form of ownership is complex but worth it for something that you think will last beyond your lifetime or that is complicated enough and/or needs protection of personal assets. This does require advisement and the filing of quarterly profit and loss statements. It can get pricey to be incorporated but if the business is successful and has the ability to do this, it should be done.

It is costly to file for incorporation and it can be complex for how to do it. I have done this before on my own but many businesses pay for a service to do this for them instead.

There are C or S type corporations and both of these should be identified and helped by your business. C is a separate entity that protects owners from personal loss. This also has to be set up as corporate profits and leads to double taxation (income taxed for the corporation and the "owners" or "shareholders").

The S-type Corporation allows you to only declare profits and loss on your personal tax return so avoiding double taxation and allowing for limited personal liability.

Again, meet with a professional to decide what is the best option for your business.

Limited Liability Company

This is similar to an S-type corporation in that you create it and run your taxes for you and the company on your 1040 but it allows for the limited liability of losses.

Incorporating allows for the ability to access more capital and can allow your business to seem more professional.

The decision of how to structure your company is a personal decision and it is based off of where your business is now and can be revisited at any time. You can start off as a sole proprietor and then decide to become a Limited Liability Company.

The next few chapters break up the business plan in mini-lessons so that you have a resource and a template in mind to begin creating your business plan. Keep in mind the business plan is a living document. It will grow and change as you continue to build your business.

Chapter 8:

Business Plan Lessons Part 1 & 2

1) **Executive summary**: High level information on your idea and how it will work. Your success factors. You will go back at the end and backfill this section with more information as you complete the business plan.

2) **Business description**: Full detail of your idea and how it will work.

Executive summary

The executive summary is done in the beginning and then usually redone at the end of the business plan. This is the case because you often come up with new ideas and plans as you continue to grow your business.

Consider the executive summary being the high level information necessary for an investor or just for you to have and be able to live by. You can then take this information and build it into your mission or vice versa. What would be the bare bones of your company description? Executive meaning the type of high level corporate executives who hate to read more than a few paragraphs. This piece is really the TLDR (too long didn't read) for the whole entire business plan. Conceivably, someone should be able to read the executive summary and now everything about your company and maybe even know if they would want to a) lend you money b) invest in you or c) hire you / partner with you based off of the document.

Take a stab at your executive summary here- remember that you will come back to it and recreate it once you complete the whole business plan.

Your Executive Summary

_____

_____

_____

_____

_____

_____

_____

_____

_____

_____

Business Description

This allows you to have more space and pages to detail all there is to know about your business, what you are selling either a product or service and how you create it.

You should consider if you need a patent – every year as a professor, I make my students design and come up with their own business. I use templates that were created in my previous life in corporate America and that revolve around using financials and marketing to come up with a business. I will include some of this information in future chapters.

Every year, my students create and design things that often times could be executed on for them to actually move forward as entrepreneurs and sometimes what they build and explain to me could qualify for patents. I always try to encourage them to patent their ideas.

During my MBA program, we came up with the wireless mouse for computers and to this day, one of our group members disappeared and we often wonder if he patented the idea and made billions- hey you never know.

Your business description should include how you plan to begin the business, where you will work out of and how you will work. It should include what you will be doing to build your idea or your products or your customer base. It should also include details around your product or service offering and specifics on how you can achieve those products and services.

Draft it here –

Your Business Description

_____

_____

_____

_____

_____

_____

_____

_____

Did you include your niche? What makes you unique? This should be addressed in both your executive summary and your business description.

As we move forward in the other pieces of the business plan, you will see how the layers work. It is like an onion – there are many many levels to a business plan and honestly the first draft of it and starting with the executive summary and business description are really the pieces that write themselves.

You do not need a lot of hand holding through these pieces because they should be what you know inside and out. It should be something you are passionate about and something you know a lot about.

No matter what, when you own your own business it becomes an all-encompassing thing no matter how you try to compartmentalize your scheduling. You will have a sense of pride and accomplishment in what you are building and with the successes that will come from learning with me on how to do this, the potential is endless!

Chapter 9:

Business Plans Lessons Part 3 & 4

3) **Market strategies and analysis**: Your description of the market should include an account of the market, its size, its trends and characteristics, and its growth rate. Describe your market research. List your competitors and describe your competitive advantage. Provide your marketing plan, your product and pricing strategies, and your plans for promotion

4) **Design and development plan**: What business structure will you use; how will you create or run your business (depending on the idea - if it is a product, how will you create it? If it is a service, how will you roll it out, etc etc).

Market Strategies and Analysis

This is basically market research. Many people cringe and run away when they hear the word "research". I get it. It feels like a paper for school but as I tell my college and career readiness clients and students in my programs that those papers can be the boost you need to stand out in the crowd as the best hire.

Same for this process- without the appropriate market research, you will fail. It is not you might fail – you will fail. You have to know who you want to attract as customers and where to find them. You have to know what the market "wants" and to be the one who can fulfill that need – or to make that want into a need.

People can forego "wants" based on finances and/or other mitigating factors but it is way harder to pass up a need. If someone needs your product or services, it makes it that much easier to attract new clients.

Of course, attracting clients is not all you have to do – you have to retain them. It is the 80/20 rule – you get 80% of your business from 20% of your clients. Also, as you have heard many times I am sure it costs more to get new clients than to keep the ones you have.

Also in terms of customer service and managing clients, if you do an amazing job, the person will maybe tell 1-2 people. If you, however, make a mistake or do a terrible job, they will tell everyone they know!

The lessons I shared in the chapter on Marketing should be included in this section (remember, the 5 P's of marketing and how you will address and manage those P's).

Think in terms of stage 1 of your start up only. Yes, you could conceivably reach the world as I mentioned earlier in the book but do you want to right now? The faster you grow, the harder it is – yes, it is an amazing thing to grow and be in demand but you must have a plan to handle that growth and demand (which I will talk about in Chapter 11).

Stay focused on stages in your development. Your first stage can be to launch in one or two towns or cities. You cannot truly predict though where your clients will come from as you build out your web presence and follow my social media plan for your new venture. Even if you are a local brick and mortar firm, people could travel to find you or could reach out to you from other places for access to your services/products.

As you grow and identify new markets, this section of your plan should be updated. You do not want to expand without knowing how to do it or how to reach the right people. If you plan on spending money for marketing (which I do not do) then you do not want to foolishly spend your marketing dollars on the wrong areas.

Knowing your competition is smart – it will help you identify and expand on your competitive advantage. For me, my competitive advantages are the fact that I am a very dynamic speaker who has been in front of the classrooms and boardrooms giving training and presentations since 1994. Also, I write books (like this one) showcasing my expertise and building out my lessons and guides to help others do what I do and to succeed, too!

By creating this section of your business plan and knowing that you will be returning to it and updating it, it makes you that much more likely to succeed in your business.

Design and Development Plan

The design and development plan includes business structure and how you will develop your business in general.

I spoke in Chapter 7 about business structures. You need to know how you will launch your business. Will you start off as a sole proprietor and then look to move to corporate status? What will be the parameters for you making the upgrade in business structure type?

How will you launch your business? Is it service offerings – how will you provide the services? Will it be in person only or a web component? Can it be done virtually?

Something I did not think about when I launched this business was the ability to create and launch online courses and training. I found the need for it and was quickly able to launch and provide an online learning environment at www.thenextstep1234.moonami.com and instant teleseminars and other exciting new ways to reach my clients.

When I identified the need and the solution for it, I went to my business plan and updated it about these new developments and methods.

You will find that things morph and change; as you are out there and finding clients through your promotional plans and word of mouth, people will ask you for things in different ways. I recently had a potential client give me ideas for new product offerings and I am updating my plan, website and offerings as I type this book.

Keep an open mind. If someone asks you to change your delivery method, do not focus on how much work it will be to move from in person to online. If someone asks you to tweak your product or service such as to add in telephone counseling and/or another piece to bundle it for a special price, think about it. Do not do it if you think it will denigrate your offerings or if it will be too close to the bone on your costs.

Know what you want to make and know what you need to make. You can prefer a 30% margin or a $300 hourly rate but can you create more value by changing that margin or lowering that hourly rate? Also, do not underpay yourself too much – know your worth and stick to your guns in terms of undercutting yourself. Even though client is king, sometimes certain clients are not worth it.

You will learn this as you go – it is a real life lesson in the clients who add value and the ones you maybe regret taking on. Try to never work for free; it can be important to get that big job to build your reputation but try to never do it for free.

Having the plan in place can help you adjust accordingly as you go from theory to reality. It is important to have your "theory" so you can test it and make adjustments as you go. Being "live" and out there means tweaking how you roll out your products and services and changing or adding new products and services based on the feedback from that market you first identified and the markets that you identify as you are live. I look forward to hearing about your markets and design and development plans!

Chapter 10:

Business Plan Lessons on Parts 5 & 6

5) **Operations and management plan**: In this part of the business plan you discuss the organizational structure of the company. You can provide profiles of key managers and, if appropriate, information about your board of directors. You can also describe how you plan to train and motivate your employees, if appropriate.

6) **Financial factors**: How you will fund your business, the mockup of financials.

Operations and Management Plan

For most new companies, this is the easiest section to do because it is just YOU. This section will hopefully be expanded and updated though as your business grows.

If possible, you should have an idea in place on how you will expand if your business takes off. I am already considering hiring people for my start up and The Next Step is less than a year old.

If you incorporate, this information is necessary. You need to think about a board of directors, especially if you are interested in receiving funding or taking out business loans / financing for your business.

You should have in mind though the structure of your company. If you are incorporating or a partnership, you might have an idea already in terms of who will do what. You might be launching with an organization plan in place because you need people to achieve your business.

Think about the culture of your company – the way you design your organization will impact the culture. Do you want lots of bosses or do you prefer to have everyone be on the same level. What will you do for training? How will you get everyone on boarded? Will you hire from day one or wait until you get to a certain amount of sales. If you could design the perfect company structure and organization, what are the role you would want filled and what are the people like that you want in those roles?

Knowing this stuff now at launch can only help you as you move forward. It really is part of the power of positive thinking, too. It allows you to envision your future in terms of what your company will look like and how you can achieve that when the time comes and you need to expand.

You might find your business stays small – this is not a bad thing. If your business is one that helps you achieve your goals and you are happy with the growth of it and able to do what you need to do in your personal life, do not force yourself to grow.

You should really identify and know your financial plan so that you know what makes your business a success and how to move forward when you want to grow.

Financial Factors

This is the crux of any business model. You need to know what you are spending on the business and what you are making. Even if you do not spend money on marketing per se you will be spending money on business swag (which I guess is part of marketing and yes, I do spend money on this). You need at a minimum business cards and it is a great idea to create some cards as a magnet and maybe to have a calendar magnet representing your business.

You also have expenses from your website – even if you start with the free version of the site to begin with in order to create an online store, you need to upgrade your site and pay money for that ability. If you instead are selling on online sites such as EBay or Etsy, you still need to manage for the fees and other costs associated with being a seller on those sites.

If you are offering a product, you need to understand all of the costs associated with creating that product so that you can charge for it appropriately so as to not wind up losing money.

If you are offering a service, you still need to identify how long it takes you to do it and what is a fair market rate for your work given your skills and talents, too.

You also need to track other expenses as tax time will be arriving either quarterly if you are incorporated or yearly if you are using your tax returns to claim the business.

When it comes to identifying and understanding financials, some business owners struggle. The best thing you could do is get a familiarity with QuickBooks (accounting software) or consider hiring a freelance bookkeeper or getting help from your accountant.

When I owned an LLC for my sports card memorabilia store I owned with my husband, we had to file quarterly statements and we had an accountant on retainer to help with that but it was my responsibility to compile the information on sales, expenses and to provide it to the accountant so they could create the filings.

It is always important to consult with a legal or tax professional to identify how you should begin your record keeping. Your online selling through EBay will be tracked and you do get a tax form if you sell more than a certain dollar amount.

Your website "store" will also be a way for you to track your sales but you want to also track your expense to offset appropriately the cost of goods sold and the investments you are making in your business.

Chapter 11:

Business Plans on Managing for Growth

Plan for Growth: Here you describe your plans to grow the business and the challenges it may face. You may also describe your plans to franchise or license the business, if that is part of its plan for growth.

Growth is awesome, it is amazing and it can be dangerous. You need to be aware of the potential for growth, just like you need to be aware of the potential for failure.

Not every business succeeds but by trying and setting up a business it will help you in the long run with skills and talents you did not know you have. Also, it provides you with a platform to discuss things in your industry or field via your blog and beyond. If you are out of work and need to fill those blank spaces on your resume, being a small business owner can help you stand apart from people who were unable to start something and just waited for a new job to come along.

While planning for growth, you should also plan for potential liquidation and/or closing of your company.

I have closed businesses that were unprofitable in the past. I learned over the past 12+ years as an entrepreneur how to succeed and by reading this book, you will be positioned to move towards the growth option and not the closing down option.

If you find, though, that running the business is not an enjoyable experience or that you are spending more money than you are making, it will be time for you to pull the plug. It can be sad but you would work with your lawyer and/or accountant to dissolve the partnership or to close out the corporation. If it is a sole proprietorship, you would just cease doing business and finish up with taxes based off of operating years only.

I prefer, though, to talk about growth. If you follow my principles and methods, you most likely will be experiencing growth. To have steady, yearly growth is actually preferable than having explosive growth.

It is just as hard to manage explosive growth as closing your business. You need to be able to scale appropriately. You need to have an idea of what you next week, 3-months, 6-months and year+ will look like in terms of demand. These will be estimations unless you take on long term projects and know you can only handle 3 for a year.

Even then, though, if you expanded and brought on more staff (or staff period), you could manage more projects and make potentially more revenues. It is a balancing decision, though and it is dependent on the pieces of your business plan and the idea in your head and heart about how your business should look, feel and run.

Growth is best if it is managed growth but you cannot really run away from the explosive growth. That being said, explosive growth requires finesse and management around how to move forward and how to maintain good client relationships.

If you become so in demand (you if a service or your product) and you cannot meet the orders you received, it can be a public relations nightmare. You need to know and understand your capabilities and how you can scale to get larger or to meet increased demand. It is important to be as transparent as possible in this regard with stakeholders and clients – so that people are aware of what you can deliver and that you never overpromise and then under deliver.

The best way to manage for growth is for gradual growth. Going with me from zero to launch means that anything can happen, though. If you follow my principles and rules that I put down in this book and the first installment of this series The Prof's Guide to Entrepreneur-ING: Using Entrepreneurial Skills to Launch a Business or Be the Boss of Your Career, then you might find yourself with a business that grows quicker than you imagined.

I will lay out in the next chapter all about how I would like to see a feedback loop instituted for this book and beyond so consider me your online small business consultant. Or maybe you got these books while taking my course in Entrepreneurship at Wagner College Department for Lifelong Learning – in that case, I am more than your online business consultant, I am your partner in this adventure!

Managing growth is a good thing but it can be too much of a good thing so be sure you have a plan in place and an understanding of what you can take on and when you have to defer and/or turn down new opportunities.

Also, knowing how you want to expand and if you want to expand are key. For me, it is like the commercial from the early 2000's where this group of business people are going into a meeting and someone asks one of their team, "Do you know what we are doing." And he points to his head and goes, "It is all in here." Moments later, he walks into an open filing cabinet drawer and is passed out while everyone on his team looks around in horror.

I liken my business model to this – I am the business. I am the speaker, the writer and the person who manages and does everything. I am working on my own plan for growth as after launching this business in July 2015, I see now how much the growth potential is as I add on new services, new markets and more. I also know I have people who are available to make my journey smoother in resources, networking partners and potential new hires.

The core of this business will always be me and my thoughts, skills and abilities but I need to transition to new models and new ways to meet demand.

This is exciting and something any small business owner needs to know. Learn with me, too, continually on my blog and my Instagram – I share the internal process of being an entrepreneur and balancing side gigs and family life, too!

Chapter 12:

Compilation on Whole Business Plan and The Next Step Resources

Once you have all of these components drafted, you are ready to move forward and launch your business.

You learned in this book how to use social media, how to build a website and how to take each piece and idea around your business to make it a living, breathing, successful venture.

You can continue to learn with me in my courses, seminars, workshops and on my blog and other books as well as through my social media channels such as Twitter, Instagram and YouTube.

I am interested in learning from you, too. It is exciting to share and meet new people so if you have read this book, provide me with feedback on what I got right and what I got wrong. Also let me know what you did with your business and how my advice and lessons helped (or did not help). I am interested in feedback in any way.

This book has the lessons and the instructional guide on how you can move forward to create this business idea you have and are interested in doing with your future career path. It can be a side gig or a full time pursuit. It can start as something you only do once a week and become your full time passion and path.

What is most important is to know your vision and to not compromise it. You have a ton to offer and the issue with promotion is knowing how to promote your business without coming on too strong. Some people will get you and your mission and they will be your biggest supporters; even if they never hire you or buy from you.

Some people will buy from you and you will wish they did not because of issues that arise. Take each interaction as a learning experience. Do not be afraid to ask for feedback. By integrating feedback into your business, you can learn what you do well and fix what you do not do well.

If you are interested in learning more and having more one on one time with me, here is the view of my course syllabus for the Entrepreneurship: Build Your Own Business Course with Wagner College Department for Lifelong Learning – you can see the book follows the course design:

Entrepreneurship: Build Your Own Business

SYLLABUS

Purpose of this Course

The global mission of this course will be to decide, complete and formulate the business plan and begin the marketing plan for your next step as an entrepreneur. This course will provide real-world strategies and advice on running your own business - from how to pick your business idea, to Web development, processing payments and other practical advice from a fellow entrepreneur.

The course is set up as 12 interactive modules and a feedback loop that will include specific readings and advice around the necessary items to launch your own business as well as real world completion of your Business Plan and draft Marketing Plan. You will have the ability to share and learn from your other cohorts as well as the Professor of the course in weekly discussion boards and at scheduled chat sessions.

You will complete the course with a professional business plan and the beginning stages of your marketing plan, including Web site development assistance and Social Media Marketing know-how. The course is taught by Professor Lisa Nielsen, Founder The Next Step (thenextstep1234.weebly.com), an entrepreneur and educator who has real world experience on how to launch a new business and taking that next step.

How the Course Will Work

This course is an online course from October 19, 2015 – April 29, 2016 and will provide the course participant with 50 continuing education hours (or 5.0 c.e.u.).

There will be PowerPoint documents and other documentation in each module representing the assignments to complete and discussion points for the group. The participants in the class will then use Moodle for group discussions – set up and moderated by the class professor. There will also be chat sessions and real world applications /edits of all documents.

 As part of the course work, students will be expected to complete a course evaluation at the completion of their work.

 Course Completion Policy: To receive a Certificate of Completion, students will be required to complete all readings, assignments, course evaluation, and participate fully in blogs, chat sessions, forums and other mediums placed on your course management system. Should you require an extension, please contact the Department for Lifelong Learning at 718-390-3221 no later than Friday, April 15, 2016. No extensions will be given after April 29th.

Course Plan and Work Requirements

There are 12 modules and a feedback loop, each requiring a specific number of hours work / instruction which will yield the 50 hours of continuing education (see chart below for information on hours per module). The course has a rolling admission so people will join in at different points; which can help re-solidify points and makes all students co-mentors and helpers of the other business owners. Building a business plan is an iterative process so this allows for the constant improvement and discussions of like-minded individuals, which will only help each cohort better develop and build their business plans, and perhaps execute on some of the items

If you join and finish the modules in the 50 hours before the end of the course, I suggest you stay part of the discussion to continue learning and improving your business plan and other materials developed during the course.

Description	Plan / amount of time to complete
Module 1: Introductions, What are your business ideas and Interests & Vision Board (Writing Your Future Exercise)	rolling admission so when enrolled, start here. Approx time to complete 5 hours
Module 2: How to Build a Website for Your Business, Quick & Dirty HTML Coding	quiz on coding / creating a cheat sheet on simple coding 3 hours
Module 3: How to Use Social Media for Your Business (Twitter, LinkedIn, Facebook, Blogging)	4 hours
Module 4: More about	2 hours

blogging	
Module 5: How to structure your business	2 hours
Module 6: Writing a business plan; Overview of the 7 pieces of the business plan and the marketing plan; Mission Statement / Mantra	4 hours
Module 7: Part 1 and 2 of your Business Plan 1) Executive summary: High level information on your idea and how it will work. Your success factors. You will go back at the end and backfill this section with more information as you complete the business plan. 2) Business description: Full detail	3 hours

of your idea and how it will work.	
Module 8:Part 3 and 4 of your Business Plan	4 hours

Module 8:Part 3 and 4 of your Business Plan (row continued below):

3) Market strategies and analysis: Your description of the market should include an account of the market, its size, its trends and characteristics, and its growth rate. Describe your market research. List your competitors and describe your competitive advantage. Provide your marketing plan, your product and pricing strategies, and your plans for promotion

4) Design and development plan: What business structure will you use; how will you create or run your business

(depending on the idea - if it is a product, how will you create it? If it is a service, how will you roll it out, etc etc).	
Module 9: Part 5 and 6 of your Business Plan 5) Operations and management plan: In this part of the business plan you discuss the organizational structure of the company. You can provide profiles of key managers and, if appropriate, information about your board of directors. You can also describe how you plan to train and motivate your employees, if appropriate. 6) Financial factors: How you will fund your business, the mock up of financials (a template will be	4 hours

provided).	
Module 10: Part 7 of your Business Plan 7) Plan for Growth: Here you describe your plans to grow the business and the challenges it may face. You may also describe your plans to franchise or license the business, if that is part of its plan for growth.	4 hours
Module 11: Draft Marketing Plan, promotion, business cards, incorporation of social media	4 hours
Module 12: Compilation of whole business plans / review and next steps	4 hours
Feedback Loop Open Questions & Answers & Next	4 hours

Steps – Case Studies	

Supplementary Text

Entrepreneurial Small Business, 14th Edition. Katz, Jeffrey

McGraw-Hill 2014

About the Professor

Lisa Nielsen is a business executive, educator and entrepreneur.

She is born and raised on Staten Island with a BS degree in Marketing and a MBA in International Finance. Her MBA is from the Rome, Italy campus of St John's University, where she learned how to speak Italian.

Upon returning to the United States, she began her career in financial services and publishing industries. Her career focus was Project Management and she became certified as a Project Management Professional from the Project Management Institute in 2004. She left Corporate America as a Vice President at Marsh, Inc where she helped manage a pipeline of over $2m in sales.

She left corporate to focus on her teaching and entrepreneurial pursuits. Lisa began teaching at the

University level in 2003 and learned she has a passion and a knack for teaching complex topics with a mix of real world and academic expertise.

Lisa has run her own businesses over the years as a consultant helping prepare business plans and helping professionals and students plan and take their next step. Her recently re-launched company, The Next Step (www.thenextstep1234.weebly.com) provides services from preparing for an interview to e-content for courses and training along with resume editing and more. Lisa is a true Renaissance woman with many strengths and loves helping her clients and students succeed.

In Closing:

Thank you so much for reading this book! Please feel free to contact me with any questions or concerns at www.thenextstep1234.com or follow me for more advice and tips on Twitter and Instagram @thenext_step123.

This book is based off of over 12 years' experience as an educator and entrepreneur in life and in teaching others how to do it. The tips and advice written are applicable to your life and your business.

I truly hope you decide to continue to learn from me and that you reach out to me with any questions via my website or email lisa@thenextstep1234.com.

If there is anything this edition did not address that you think future editions should, please let me know. If you did not agree with something or think I need to add more to included topics, let me know that, too. Writing is something you do alone but you want to have people who read it impacted and/or provide feedback so please feel free to let me know what you think!

Happy Hunting!

Previously published books by Lisa Vento Nielsen

The Prof's Guide to Entrepreneur-ing – Using Entrepreneurial Skills to Launch Your Own Business or be the Boss of Your Career

The Book on College Readiness The Prof's Guide to Surviving High School and Kicking Butt in College *(First in a series on College & Career Readiness)*

The Book on Career Readiness – The Prof's Guide on How to Graduate with a Job Offer

Books in progress by Lisa Vento Nielsen:

The Book on Career Readiness Part 2 – How to Manage Your Career as a New Professional

How to Blog Like a Pro-Fessor

www.ingramcontent.com/pod-product-compliance
Lightning Source LLC
Chambersburg PA
CBHW060352190526
45169CB00002B/569